★ ★ ★ ★ ★ ★ ★ ★ ★ ★ ★ ★

YOU MAY BE

40

But You've Still

GOT IT

★ ★ ★ ★ ★ ★ ★ ★ ★ ★ ★ ★

summersdale

YOU MAY BE 40 BUT YOU'VE STILL GOT IT

Summersdale Publishers Ltd
46 West Street
Chichester
West Sussex
PO19 1RP
UK

www.summersdale.com

Printed and bound in China

ISBN: 978-1-84953-347-8

Substantial discounts on bulk quantities of Summersdale books are available to corporations, professional associations and other organisations. For details telephone Nicky Douglas on (+44-1243-756902), fax (+44-1243-786300) or email (nicky@summersdale.com).

To...

From..

★ ★ ★ ★ ★ ★ ★ ★ ★ ★ ★ ★ ★

NO MAN IS HAPPY WHO DOES NOT THINK HIMSELF SO.

PUBLILIUS SYRUS

★ ★ ★ ★ ★ ★ ★ ★ ★ ★ ★ ★ ★

★ ★ ★ ★ ★ ★ ★ ★ ★ ★ ★ ★

Treat yourself like *royalty* for a day: make a luxury breakfast, have a long bath, book yourself a massage, concoct a *decadent cocktail* and do all the little things you enjoy.

★ ★ ★ ★ ★ ★ ★ ★ ★ ★ ★ ★

Go on one **_wild night out_**
with your friends wearing an
outfit you would otherwise
have **_thrown away_**
because 'I can't pull this
off any more.'

★ ★ ★ ★ ★ ★ ★ ★ ★ ★ ★ ★ ★

★ ★ ★ ★ ★ ★ ★ ★ ★ ★ ★ ★

Master a **skill.** You are probably already very good at some things, but by focusing intensely on improving one of them further you can become an *expert* in that field.

★ ★ ★ ★ ★ ★ ★ ★ ★ ★ ★ ★

* * * * * * * * * * * * *

Get a **trampoline** for
your garden. It'll help you
stay in shape and is
lots of fun.

* * * * * * * * * * * * *

★ ★ ★ ★ ★ ★ ★

LIVE, LAUGH AND LOVE.

★ ★ ★ ★ ★ ★ ★

★ ★ ★ ★ ★ ★ ★ ★ ★ ★ ★ ★ ★ ★

This summer, try a new type of holiday. If you usually sit on a beach with a book and a mojito, why not try staying in a hostel out in the sticks; if you normally stay in a rented cottage in the country, try **snowboarding** in the Alps to spice things up.

★ ★ ★ ★ ★ ★ ★ ★ ★ ★ ★ ★ ★

* * * * * * * * * * * *

Send a *care package* to
a friend in need to cheer
them up – it could be sweets,
flowers, a film for them to
enjoy or a good book you
think they *will love.*

* * * * * * * * * * * *

Adopt an outrageous new *hobby;* whether it's unicycle riding, belly dancing or taxidermy, now is the perfect time to *give it a go!*

★ ★ ★ ★ ★ ★ ★ ★ ★ ★ ★ ★ ★

WHEN IN DOUBT, SMILE.

★ ★ ★ ★ ★ ★ ★ ★ ★ ★ ★

Dedicate an afternoon to perfecting that *gourmet* meal which will become your *pièce de résistance...*

★ ★ ★ ★ ★ ★ ★ ★ ★ ★ ★

… or if your cooking skills aren't quite up to scratch, you could try out this extra-special recipe for *beans on toast:*

★ Chop and fry an onion and a garlic clove, add the beans and bring to a simmer.

★ Add grilled and crumbled bacon and chilli sauce.

★ Spoon the beans over two slices of buttered toast.

★ Sprinkle grated cheese on top. Cheddar works well, but you can choose any cheese.

Watch a song from the eighties on **YouTube** that you remember *really really* hating at the time, to see if you still feel the *same way.*

★ ★ ★ ★ ★ ★ ★ ★ ★ ★ ★ ★ ★

★ ★ ★ ★ ★ ★ ★ ★ ★ ★ ★ ★

Buy a beautiful **notebook,** and use it to write or draw something every day. It could be something that's happened to you, a conversation you had, something you saw on TV, or even a poem about your day. You'll **look back** on it in years to come and remember this time with affection.

★ ★ ★ ★ ★ ★ ★ ★ ★ ★ ★ ★

* * * * * * * * * * * *

WE'RE FOOLS WHETHER WE DANCE OR NOT, SO WE MIGHT AS WELL DANCE.

JAPANESE PROVERB

* * * * * * * * * * * *

* * * * * * * * * * * * *

Sleep in a **tent** in the garden – it will make you feel like a **child again!**

* * * * * * * * * * * * *

Research **cocktails** that tickle your fancy, buy yourself a cocktail shaker, and master the art of the bartender – it's sure to impress at ***parties!***

★ ★ ★ ★ ★ ★ ★ ★ ★ ★ ★ ★

Next time you're walking along your local high street, **look up.** The chances are that the original shop signs, odd features and unique buildings are more *interesting* than the shops you were headed to.

★ ★ ★ ★ ★ ★ ★ ★ ★ ★ ★

Arrange your *photos.* Dig out all the old snapshots you've taken over the years and spend some time organising them into albums. Then you can show the *albums* off to friends and family.

FORTUNE
FAVOURS THE
BRAVE.

★ ★ ★ ★ ★ ★ ★ ★ ★ ★ ★ ★

Next time there's a special occasion, *treat yourself* and your partner or closest friend to the most expensive meal or bottle of wine on the menu at your *favourite restaurant.*

★ ★ ★ ★ ★ ★ ★ ★ ★ ★ ★ ★

Take part in a **_carnival_**
parade. You can ride on a
float, dance, or be part of a
huge tomato fight!

★ ★ ★ ★ ★ ★ ★ ★ ★ ★ ★ ★

* * * * * * * * * * * *

Find a new, free **sport**
to take up. There are
hundreds of free tennis
courts around the country,
fields to play football on,
parks with basketball hoops
and riverbanks, beaches
and roads just dying to be
jogged on.

* * * * * * * * * * * *

★ ★ ★ ★ ★ ★ ★ ★ ★ ★ ★ ★ ★

Gather together all the
things around the house you
don't need, be it kitchen
gadgets gathering dust
or those 'maybe one day'
trousers in your wardrobe,
and **_give them away_**
to people who will make
good use of them.

★ ★ ★ ★ ★ ★ ★ ★ ★ ★ ★ ★ ★

★ ★ ★ ★ ★ ★ ★ ★ ★ ★

MAKE FRIENDS WITH THE WORLD.

★ ★ ★ ★ ★ ★ ★ ★ ★ ★

Every day for a month, put all your **_spare change_** in a pot when you get home. At the end of the month, use the money to **_treat_** your closest friends to tea and cake, or spend your savings on a spa treatment or gig ticket for yourself.

★ ★ ★ ★ ★ ★ ★ ★ ★ ★ ★ ★

★ ★ ★ ★ ★ ★ ★ ★ ★ ★ ★ ★ ★

Get in touch with
your *spiritual* and
philosophical side, be it
by practising meditation,
reading Descartes or visiting
a place of *worship*.

★ ★ ★ ★ ★ ★ ★ ★ ★ ★ ★ ★ ★

Spend one whole day
watching all your favourite
childhood films –
enjoy the time and don't let
yourself feel *guilty*
about it.

⋆ ⋆ ⋆ ⋆ ⋆ ⋆ ⋆ ⋆ ⋆ ⋆ ⋆ ⋆

★ ★ ★ ★ ★ ★ ★ ★ ★ ★ ★ ★

Donate an evening
(one per week, if you can)
to **teaching** somebody
else one of your skills.
Whether it's teaching
young offenders to read or
teaching a friend how to
knit, it will be **enjoyable**
for everyone involved.

★ ★ ★ ★ ★ ★ ★ ★ ★ ★ ★ ★

★ ★ ★ ★ ★ ★ ★ ★ ★ ★ ★ ★

THE JOURNEY OF A THOUSAND MILES BEGINS WITH ONE STEP.

LAO TZU

★ ★ ★ ★ ★ ★ ★ ★ ★ ★ ★ ★

Try a *national cuisine* that you've never eaten before. Depending on how you're feeling, you can either try to make it yourself or *eat out.*

* * * * * * * * * * * * *

* * * * * * * * * * *

Teach yourself to *juggle:*
there are plenty of how-to
videos on the *Internet.*

* * * * * * * * * * *

Invite all your friends to
ballroom dancing
lessons so that you can learn
to dance **_like the stars._**

★ ★ ★ ★ ★ ★ ★ ★ ★ ★ ★ ★ ★ ★

Go to an **open mic** night
and embrace your inner
superstar! You could
learn a simple song on the
acoustic guitar, sing to a
backing track, or do a short
comedy routine. Get a friend
to join you for moral support.

★ ★ ★ ★ ★ ★ ★ ★ ★ ★ ★ ★

★ ★ ★ ★ ★ ★ ★

IT IS YOUR STRENGTHS, NOT YOUR WEAKNESSES, THAT DEFINE WHO YOU ARE.

★ ★ ★ ★ ★ ★ ★

★ ★ ★ ★ ★ ★ ★ ★ ★ ★ ★ ★

On a cold day, make a batch of **soup** and feed your friends or colleagues. On a hot day, make a batch of *fruit smoothies* to share amongst your co-workers.

★ ★ ★ ★ ★ ★ ★ ★ ★ ★ ★ ★

Take a long weekend off work to go **backpacking** – be it at home or in foreign lands, with friends or alone, getting back in touch with *nature* can do wonders.

★ ★ ★ ★ ★ ★ ★ ★ ★ ★ ★ ★ ★

Spend your weekly coffee allowance on **shares** in your favourite company, or product. Even if it fails, the excitement of watching their value change on the stock exchange is a *thrill* like no other.

★ ★ ★ ★ ★ ★ ★ ★ ★ ★ ★ ★

★ ★ ★ ★ ★ ★ ★ ★ ★ ★ ★ ★

A LIFE
UNCHALLENGED
IS A LIFE
NOT LIVED.

★ ★ ★ ★ ★ ★ ★ ★ ★ ★ ★ ★

★ ★ ★ ★ ★ ★ ★ ★ ★ ★ ★ ★ ★

Host a **cookery party:** get everyone to bring along a recipe and the necessary ingredients, and then all pitch in to make the *dish.* This works best with three or four people each bringing either a starter, a main or a dessert.

★ ★ ★ ★ ★ ★ ★ ★ ★ ★ ★ ★

Send a **Valentine's card** to your secret love – you could even **take the plunge** and sign your name at the bottom!

* * * * * * * * * * * *

Treat yourself to some
aromatherapy or
massage oils, and entice
your partner into helping
you ***ease away*** the
strains of the week.

* * * * * * * * * * * *

Use free **online lectures** and courses to teach yourself about a subject you feel strongly about: global warming, *human rights* or conservation are good starting points.

DON'T WORRY, BE SILLY.

★ ★ ★ ★ ★ ★ ★ ★ ★ ★ ★ ★ ★

Have **dessert** first. You're
40 now, who's going to
stop you?

★ ★ ★ ★ ★ ★ ★ ★ ★ ★ ★ ★ ★

✮ ✮ ✮ ✮ ✮ ✮ ✮ ✮ ✮ ✮ ✮ ✮ ✮

Hire a *glitzy car*
for the day, and see how
many people you can
convince that you have
won the lottery.

✮ ✮ ✮ ✮ ✮ ✮ ✮ ✮ ✮ ✮ ✮ ✮ ✮

* * * * * * * * * * * *

Reconnect with old school
friends you've lost touch
with, and find out what
they're **up to now.**

* * * * * * * * * * * *

★ ★ ★ ★ ★ ★ ★ ★

A CHANGE IS AS GOOD AS A REST.

★ ★ ★ ★ ★ ★ ★

Go on a **road trip.**
Take a picnic in the car,
and drive somewhere you've
never been. Take as many
loved ones with you as
will fit in the car.

★ ★ ★ ★ ★ ★ ★ ★ ★ ★ ★ ★

Sign up for a
charity event – a walk,
run, swim or even skydive!
Not only will you be raising
money for a ***good cause,***
but you'll reap huge benefits
for yourself as well.

* * * * * * * * * * * *

For one day (or longer
if you like!), tell everyone
you meet one thing you
really like about them:
a new shirt, their smile, their
positive attitude, their
determination – ***being nice***
won't cost you anything, and
will make you feel good.

* * * * * * * * * * * *

Dress up for work. If you usually go into the office wearing jeans and a T-shirt, opt instead for a glamorous dress or a smart suit, and wear it *with pride.*

★ ★ ★ ★ ★ ★ ★ ★ ★ ★ ★

* * * * * * * * * * *

GENIUS IS ONE PER CENT INSPIRATION, NINETY-NINE PER CENT PERSPIRATION.

THOMAS EDISON

* * * * * * * * * * *

Learn one *joke* or story that
you can tell at any social
event to *entertain*
your friends.

★ ★ ★ ★ ★ ★ ★ ★ ★ ★ ★ ★

★ ★ ★ ★ ★ ★ ★ ★ ★ ★ ★ ★

Go to a *charity shop* and pick up the first CD you see that you don't already own. Take it home and listen to it – you might discover a new *favourite band!*

★ ★ ★ ★ ★ ★ ★ ★ ★ ★ ★ ★

★ ★ ★ ★ ★ ★ ★ ★ ★ ★ ★ ★

For one evening every week, make *a pact* with your family, friends or housemates, that instead of watching TV or spending the evening at your computer, you will go for *a walk together,* cook a meal together, or simply sit and talk over a glass of wine.

★ ★ ★ ★ ★ ★ ★ ★ ★ ★ ★ ★

If you're single, try
speed dating. Go with
friends, or arrange to meet
some at the pub afterwards,
to *laugh* about it (or
hopefully, to tell them
how well it went!).

★ ★ ★ ★ ★ ★ ★ ★ ★ ★ ★ ★

★ ★ ★ ★ ★ ★ ★

SPREAD
A LITTLE
HAPPINESS.

★ ★ ★ ★ ★ ★ ★

★ ★ ★ ★ ★ ★ ★ ★ ★ ★ ★ ★

Pick a bunch of
wild flowers (but not
from private land) and
arrange them in a vase.
They'll **_brighten up_** any
room without costing a
penny; just make sure they're
not a protected species!

★ ★ ★ ★ ★ ★ ★ ★ ★ ★ ★ ★

✶ ✶ ✶ ✶ ✶ ✶ ✶ ✶ ✶ ✶ ✶ ✶

Have a chat with a neighbour you've never spoken to before when you cross paths on the stairs or in the garden. Perhaps invite them for tea! You could **make their day,** or you could make a new friend.

✶ ✶ ✶ ✶ ✶ ✶ ✶ ✶ ✶ ✶ ✶ ✶

★ ★ ★ ★ ★ ★ ★ ★ ★ ★ ★ ★

Join **Project365** at www.365project.org: an initiative that encourages its members to take a photo every day for a year. They could be snapshots of standout moments, or they could document the routines of your ***day-to-day life.***

★ ★ ★ ★ ★ ★ ★ ★ ★ ★ ★ ★

If you've never done it before, try **making sushi.** All you need is some sushi rice (stickier than regular rice), nori (sheets of seaweed), a bamboo rolling mat and whatever filling *you fancy.*

⭑ ⭑ ⭑ ⭑ ⭑ ⭑ ⭑ ⭑ ⭑ ⭑ ⭑ ⭑

★ ★ ★ ★ ★ ★ ★ ★ ★ ★ ★

LIFE IS
SWEET.

★ ★ ★ ★ ★ ★ ★ ★ ★ ★ ★

Join a club – whether it's creative writing, debating, walking or jogging, you're bound to make new friends and have a ***good time!***

Buy a ***musical instrument*** (new or second-hand) and make a commitment to ***learning*** to play at least five songs on it.

★ ★ ★ ★ ★ ★ ★ ★ ★ ★ ★

★ ★ ★ ★ ★ ★ ★ ★ ★ ★ ★ ★

Wake up 30 minutes earlier than usual and spend the time doing one of the things you never seem to find the time for – be it rereading a favourite book or taking up jogging. You'll feel more ***productive*** and get the day off to a great start.

★ ★ ★ ★ ★ ★ ★ ★ ★ ★ ★ ★

* * * * * * * * * * *

Go *camping* with friends, and toast marshmallows over a campfire. Keep your mobile phone packed away, only to be used in emergencies, and use as *little technology* as is possible.

* * * * * * * * * * *

★ ★ ★ ★ ★ ★

TODAY IS THE FIRST DAY OF THE REST OF YOUR LIFE.

★ ★ ★ ★ ★ ★ ★

★ ★ ★ ★ ★ ★ ★ ★ ★ ★ ★ ★

Get that extreme **haircut**
you never dared try in your
twenties. Who says those
young folk should have
all the fun?

★ ★ ★ ★ ★ ★ ★ ★ ★ ★ ★ ★

Volunteer to help out
in your community, be it at
a school, an old people's
home, or a *charity event.*

★ ★ ★ ★ ★ ★ ★ ★ ★ ★ ★ ★

★ ★ ★ ★ ★ ★ ★ ★ ★ ★ ★ ★ ★

Surprise your partner with a *'memory lane'* date night – go to the place you first met, had your *first date,* or shared your first kiss, and relive all your wonderful memories together.

★ ★ ★ ★ ★ ★ ★ ★ ★ ★ ★ ★ ★

✦ ✦ ✦ ✦ ✦ ✦ ✦ ✦ ✦ ✦ ✦

Just this **once,** go out for
the **evening** when you've
got work the next day.

✦ ✦ ✦ ✦ ✦ ✦ ✦ ✦ ✦ ✦ ✦

★ ★ ★ ★ ★ ★ ★ ★ ★ ★ ★ ★

EVER TRIED. EVER FAILED. NO MATTER. TRY AGAIN. FAIL AGAIN. FAIL BETTER.

SAMUEL BECKETT

★ ★ ★ ★ ★ ★ ★ ★ ★ ★ ★ ★

Send a message in
a bottle; who knows who
will find your *little note!*

★ ★ ★ ★ ★ ★ ★ ★ ★ ★ ★ ★

★ ★ ★ ★ ★ ★ ★ ★ ★ ★ ★ ★

If you always wanted
to but never learnt to
ride a bike, dance
like a pro or speak a
foreign language, it's
never too late to try —
ask a friend to teach you,
get a self-help book or
enrol in evening classes.

★ ★ ★ ★ ★ ★ ★ ★ ★ ★ ★ ★

Find your local
climbing wall or
adventure park and book
a weekend break with some
friends — not only will it be
a fun and different way to
spend your free time, but
being active is great for
your health and your heart.

★ ★ ★ ★ ★ ★ ★ ★ ★ ★ ★

★ ★ ★ ★ ★ ★ ★ ★ ★ ★

MAKE EVERY MOMENT COUNT.

★ ★ ★ ★ ★ ★ ★ ★ ★ ★

Buy yourself some
extravagant new **bedding,**
from pillowcases and
duvet-covers to quilts and
runners, so that you can
sleep like a king.

★ ★ ★ ★ ★ ★ ★ ★ ★ ★ ★

★ ★ ★ ★ ★ ★ ★ ★ ★ ★ ★ ★

Go to a *car boot sale*
with some friends, decide
on an amount of money you
want to spend and a time
and place to meet. Divide
up, and go hunting for the
perfect gift to give
one of the group.

★ ★ ★ ★ ★ ★ ★ ★ ★ ★ ★ ★

Be a *tourist* in your own town or city. Visit the local museums and places of interest that take your fancy. *Take a camera* with you and document the whole day. You'll see a whole new side of the place you call 'home'.

* * * * * * * * * * * *

★ ★ ★ ★ ★ ★ ★ ★ ★ ★ ★ ★

Confront *your fears:* whatever it is that frightens you most in life (with the notable exceptions of death or pain), *try it.* If you're scared of heights, go to the top of the tallest building you know. If you're scared of spiders, visit the insect house at your local zoo.

★ ★ ★ ★ ★ ★ ★ ★ ★ ★ ★ ★

★ ★ ★ ★ ★ ★ ★ ★ ★ ★ ★ ★

Plant some fruit, veg or herbs in window boxes (or in a garden or allotment if you have one) and when they are grown, **make a meal** out of all your home-grown food to share with friends and family.

★ ★ ★ ★ ★ ★ ★ ★ ★ ★ ★ ★

* * * * * * * * * * * * *

For a day, do all your
errands on *roller skates.*
But maybe put in some
practice first, if you need it
– and wear protective knee
and *elbow pads!*

* * * * * * * * * * * * *

★ ★ ★ ★ ★ ★ ★ ★ ★ ★ ★ ★

Find the perfect *bridge* to play *Poohsticks.*

★ ★ ★ ★ ★ ★ ★ ★ ★ ★ ★ ★

★ ★ ★ ★ ★ ★ ★ ★ ★ ★ ★ ★

Send an *email* to an old
friend to let them know
you're *thinking of them.*

★ ★ ★ ★ ★ ★ ★ ★ ★ ★ ★ ★

★ ★ ★ ★ ★ ★ ★ ★ ★ ★ ★

HAPPINESS BEGETS HAPPINESS IN OTHERS

– SMILE!

★ ★ ★ ★ ★ ★ ★ ★ ★ ★ ★

Book a few days **off work,**
go to the airport, and
book yourself onto the next
available (affordable!) flight,
no matter the destination.
Investigate a *new culture,*
and make as many friends
as you can.

★ ★ ★ ★ ★ ★ ★ ★ ★ ★ ★ ★

Hold a themed
fancy dress party
for your birthday or just
because you want to. Make
sure you put lots of effort
into your ***costume.***

★ ★ ★ ★ ★ ★ ★ ★ ★ ★ ★

✶ ✶ ✶ ✶ ✶ ✶ ✶ ✶ ✶ ✶ ✶ ✶

Attach brightly coloured
streamers and bells
to your bike, and ride
through town.

✶ ✶ ✶ ✶ ✶ ✶ ✶ ✶ ✶ ✶ ✶ ✶

Look forward to what you hope to have achieved and *experienced* by your fiftieth birthday.

* * * * * * * * * * * *

THERE IS ONLY
ONE PERSON WHO
COULD EVER MAKE
YOU HAPPY, AND
THAT PERSON
IS YOU.

DAVID BURNS

* * * * * * * * * * * *

If you're interested in finding out more
about our gift books, follow us on Twitter:
@Summersdale

www.summersdale.com